Reflections of a Beret

teven ates

Reflections of a Beret

2nd edition

For more information see:
www.facebook.com/StevenBatesMusings
www.facebook.com/ForgottenPlacesPublishing
or
www.forgottenplacespublishing.com

Follow Steven Bates on twitter: @StevenBatesPoet

Forgotten Places Publishing
2200 Park Pl
Cheyenne, WY 82001

ISBN: 978-1-944621-10-0

DEDICATION

To those who supported me, without you I would have not made it to where I am today.

CONTENTS

ACKNOWLEDGMENTS

As I sit at my desk typing this dedication, and after painstakingly going page by page tweaking words here or spaces there, I have found there are so many persons who have encouraged me over the years. I couldn't possibly name, much less remember, them all. There are those who have stood out, giving me much more than simple encouragement. Those are the ones I hope to mention here.

It might have taken me in the neighborhood of 35 years or more in the making –since I penned my first poem in high school– but with the encouragement and love so many others have given me, I finally have gone to print.

There are only a few minutes in one's life out of the millions of minutes in a lifetime one can honestly say has made a difference: the birth of a child, the breath of life in a lifeless body, the fatal shot ringing out through the night, and the words *I do*; and many more. My life was profoundly impacted by each of my children being born, whether they know it or not. My goal in life became the desire to hand my children something, anything, that they could be proud of their father accomplishing. This book is something tangible they can hold in their hands and say, "My dad made this," or "my father did that." I know all my children have been positive and supportive about my writing, especially my eldest Ashley and my youngest Zavier. But I want all my children to eventually have the same respect for their father as I have for mine.

My father, now in his late 70s, can still out work many young men in their prime. His persistence, morals, faith, and perseverance are so strong, I often feel like a disappointment when comparing life accomplishments. My mother and father not only encouraged me in my writing, but have done more to impact my belief system than they shall ever know. I love you Mom and Dad. Thanks for being there, even when I wasn't.

My wife, Sandy, is perhaps the most incredible and beautiful woman I know. In being such an amazing person, she fails to realize that her eyes alone grant me the strength to persist in this venture. Her words of encouragement fill me with the inspiration often needed to press on, no matter how lousy I feel about one of my poems. She, as good ol' Jack Nicholson once said, makes me want to be a better person; and subsequently, a better poet. I would be remiss if I didn't tell her I love her in this dedication, although she knows it quite well. I love you Sandy, forever and ever, always, no matter what!

There are so many others, through direct or indirect words, have given me the desire and drive to put all 35 years of writing into one collection. A big thanks to all those who have encouraged me in my life. From high school friends, David and Terri White, Chris Holt, and many others, to those who served with me in various units around the world, I thank you. Master Sergeants Cal Steward, Chuck O'Brian, and Deb Herndon were instrumental in shaping a young airman into the man, and writer, I would eventually become. Many thanks as well to those in the Veterans Affairs Creative Arts Program such as Kristi Ruben, Peter Bourret, Scott "Papa Bear" Owen and Don Harmon who also influenced my decision to continue writing and eventually publish.

My wife's father, Larry Elling, didn't meet me until a few years before his passing. During that first meeting, he appeared to judge me to be something he found off-putting. In time though, I learned a lot about him. After I got my ponytail and beard trimmed, he learned a lot of me and eventually we had many discussions of his life and many careers. I respected him for the wonderful daughter he had blessed my life with, and for the "stick to it" attitude he possessed regarding ethics and morals. Larry earned a special place in my heart and for that, I have placed my poem of tribute to him as the last poem in my book. I wrote that piece shortly after his passing and read it to his family and loved ones at his funeral. It is only fitting that the book closes with the closing of one's chapter among the living.

Thank you, Larry. It was an honor.

WAR

THE GRASSHOPPER
(written during Desert Shield)

I watched a grasshopper
'Neath my feet at my post,
as he enjoyed the sunshine
Of this nation, his host.

The wind blew his body
as he fought hard to stand still,
But he stood nonetheless
With what seemed like sheer will.

And I thought to myself,
as alone I oft do.
How I wish, little grasshopper,
that I could be like you.

Without knowledge of nuclear,
or chemical wars
Or of blistering agents,
and their unsightly sores.

Without knowledge of fear,
and death coming my way
How I wish, small grasshopper,
I could be you for a day.

THOUGHTS AND REFLECTIONS

_____

_____

_____

_____

_____

_____

_____

_____

_____

_____

_____

_____

_____

_____

_____

_____

THE HARD PART OF WAR
(written during Desert Shield)

The hard part of war,
as I've heard someone say,
Is not killing, but waiting,
    for day after day.

And watching the distance,
    for just one small sign.
Or listening to night skies,
    for a jet engine's whine.

A Purple Heart they will give
    for blood spilled in a war
And for those that don't make it
    A Cross, Flag, and more.

But what of the others,
Who from stress will die young?
Who never stood with their brothers,
    or fired their guns.

But they stood nonetheless,
    and let stress eat away
From waiting and watching
And NOT fighting each day.

They are still just as brave,
    Still warriors inside.
But there will be no medallions
    To pin on their hide

And they've nothing to show,
    but their memories and pain
And a constant desire
    to *Really* fight once again.

THOUGHTS AND REFLECTIONS

WHY?
(written during Desert Shield)

Using shadows and planes
To block heat and dry wind
We wait ever patient,
For Saddam to descend.

We hope that he won't.
But think that he will
And I know if he does
We'll have Iraqi to kill.

The Saudis, Egyptians,
The British, the Yanks
Australians and Russians,
We'll cover his flanks.

With Israel to help us
We'll take Saddam down
To help all Kuwaiti
To regain their crown

Yes, we'll all join together
To help save this small nation.
So why can't we do this,
To help end World Starvation?

THOUGHTS AND REFLECTIONS

INBOUND

Sounds of popping from a distant gun
With nowhere to hide, nowhere to run
Incoming missile sirens pierce thru the night
With an enemy inbound you can't see to fight

Patriot missiles firing as fast as they can
To save us all to the very last man
Chemical suits on, eyes searching the skies
"one rocket inbound!" another voice decries

Hunker down, Bunker down, run, duck and hide
Only so much to do in this eight second ride
With moments to go you start praying to heaven
A quick little prayer and the time is now seven

Six seconds left, pray that you'll stay alive
As you think of your children the time passes to five
Four seconds to impact, death's comet bearing down
Your unfinished life brings your face to a frown

With three seconds left, you swear you'll be better
And praying your wife won't be getting that letter
Two seconds to go, there's a flash in the sky
As outbound missiles catch the bird on the fly

One second left, but the fear now has gone
As debris from the meeting reflects the new dawn.

THOUGHTS AND REFLECTIONS

_____

_____

_____

_____

_____

_____

_____

_____

_____

_____

_____

_____

_____

_____

_____

_____

_____

PRAYERS IN THE SAND

Your weary head on hardened stone
Body nestled in the sand
Above the desert noises drone
And a gun lays in your hand

Sleep, though precious, won't come tonight
For the nightmares will instead
And a memory, like a flash of light
Of the last time spent in bed

Praying silently while still you lay
That your life you'll not have to give
Though a sacrifice might be called today
And you may die, so others live

And if fate deems that give you must, And
from war your soul will roam
May faith in whichever God you trust Safely
guide your spirit home

THOUGHTS AND REFLECTIONS

_____

_____

_____

_____

_____

_____

_____

_____

_____

_____

_____

_____

_____

_____

_____

_____

_____

_____

EYES

Soulless eyes stare into space
And give a thousand-yard stare
Haunted eyes that death has graced
Eyes that no longer care

Tears dried as rivers carved thru dust
Adorn the now still cheeks
As now the soul has gone to trust
To whichever God he speaks

Vacant eyes glare back at me
As if searching who to blame
When death went on its' killing spree
And snuffed out my partner's flame

Darkness filling pupils wide
As if they seem to say
I've got this friend, now step aside
And live another day

THOUGHTS AND REFLECTIONS

_____

_____

_____

_____

_____

_____

_____

_____

_____

_____

_____

_____

_____

_____

_____

_____

THE OATH

A solemn oath you took one day
That your life you might just forfeit
In hopes a soul whose life you may
From death have given respite

To grant that life from fate a stay
For a week, a month, a decade
Or however long death's held at bay
From the actions that you made

For if one day those actions save
Another woman, child, or man
And in doing so your life you gave
As if in some cosmic plan

Remember the oath and fear not death
Or your loved one's pain and sorrow
For because of you a life took a breath,
And lived to see tomorrow

THOUGHTS AND REFLECTIONS

UNDER NINETEEN

Hand held high as oath was taken
Contracts signed as life forsaken
Past life gone as service began
"Pick 'em up, put 'em down," his first command

Hair shaved down to barely a stubble
Every experience made on the double
Uniforms ironed with crispy clean crease
Preparing for war yet training for peace

First duty assignment, so overwhelming
Adapting to rules and slowly conforming
Learning the ropes, or to him it seemed
Then a hostile event in lands he'd not dreamed

His bags packed up quickly, his rifle is clean
As he heads to new lands in his first flying machine
The sand and the wind a harsh weather change
As he proceeds with his unit somewhere down range

Hostile encounter caught all by surprise
Now he lays on his back looking up at the skies
Rushed to the medic, no hope is foreseen
Then he fulfilled his contract...
and he was just under nineteen

THOUGHTS AND REFLECTIONS

WHO DECIDES?

A stoic young soldier stands in his foxhole
Waiting ....watching...watching some more
Ever vigilant should an enemy approach
Suddenly a shadow in the dune's darkness moves

Alerted now ... all senses active...
Looking ...listening... tasting the wind like a snake
Gently caressing his trigger as he sniffs ...smelling danger
Smelling the sweat of his stalker
with his own unwashed body

Eyes piercing thru the void as the shadow inches closer
He follows directives and issues the challenge
The shadow stiffens ... frozen in its' tracks
From the waist of the entity swings an arm

The solder watches helpless as a small sphere of death flies
The grenade lands only inches away
Bursting into projectiles that shred flesh in a flash of light
The soldier ducks deeper into his refuge....

Showered by sand and shrapnel he survives
Shoot or don't shoot races thru his mind
He emerges from the sandy shower and aims
The shadow stands before him,
reveling in his imagined victory

No weapon in sight...
The shadow turns and slithers silently into the dunes
Rules of engagement saying he is no longer a threat
But yet... Is he?... And who decides?

THOUGHTS AND REFLECTIONS

_____

_____

_____

_____

_____

_____

_____

_____

_____

_____

_____

_____

_____

_____

_____

_____

_____

SURVIVOR'S GUILT

(An attempt at a sonnet)

I watched but nothing could I do to help
Too far away was I to render aid
I saw the blast , and heard his meager yelp
the instant light and sound a crater made

So now I ache, for me it should have been
my guilt so strong for making it unharmed
it grows so deep and dark I know not when
my life became so blessed with luck and charmed

Yet though I lived, my thoughts return to why
heaven spared my life and took another
He was a friend, a truly standup guy
loving father, husband, son and brother

Yet I survived to live another day
my life was spared it seems for guilt to stay

THOUGHTS AND REFLECTIONS

_____

_____

_____

_____

_____

_____

_____

_____

_____

_____

_____

_____

_____

_____

_____

_____

_____

A SOLDIER'S SONNET

The air seems alive with bullets flying
as angry mosquitoes swarming around
picking at their prey as they lay dying,
a feeding frenzy for those on the ground.

While whistles warning by their high pitched song
piercing the air with pointed teeth of steel
pressing men down as slowly they move strong
into the fray, their hearts with fervent zeal

The thund'rous echoes sounding out alarm
as hungry mortar rounds begin their fall
seeking sheltered soldiers to rain down harm
as to insure that fighters give their all

The very force of combat feeds the air
But our men stand strong and brave, without fear

THOUGHTS AND REFLECTIONS

_____

_____

_____

_____

_____

_____

_____

_____

_____

_____

_____

_____

_____

_____

_____

_____

STEVEN BATES

WAR COMES HOME (PTSD)

INSIDE MY MIND

Inside my mind, my thoughts run free
in battles no one else can see
in fighting for a cause that's right
with demons taunting through the night

Throughout the day that fear remains
though hidden, it prevails and reigns
It makes me look behind each door
always searching, forever more

Forever fearing that my old foe
hides wherever shadows grow
My scars and demons, though none can see
are within my mind, and still run free

THOUGHTS AND REFLECTIONS

_____

_____

_____

_____

_____

_____

_____

_____

_____

_____

_____

_____

_____

_____

_____

FIVE SENSES OF A VETERAN

I've seen things no man should see
and heard the screams that haunted me

I've tasted death with a kiss of life
and touched the pulse of the afterlife

I've smelled the stench of the slipped away
and cried when death has claimed its' prey

I've served in ways I can't describe
for fear of rambling in diatribe.

I survived it all and lived to tell
what life is like in earthly hell

And though my dreams still show the strain
I'd live it all, each day of pain
I'd fight the evil, the sick, depraved
to know just once, a life I saved

THOUGHTS AND REFLECTIONS

STEVEN BATES

WHAT WE NEED

Suicidal, homicidal, danger to all
That's what they call us, those that answered the call

They can't comprehend the dedication to serve
The guns and the fighting are all they observe
They don't understand, peace, our primary goal
Is that which we stand for, deep down in our soul

We help oppressed persons, those needing a hand
We help them return to their homes and their land
We help those in need, we help those put out
We help to spread freedom in countries throughout

Our mission's not killing, our goal is to defend
Yet somehow there's those who can't comprehend
We come back from war, from combat and strife
And try to assimilate, to have a good life

But our mindset has changed, and not for the good
Battling evil has made us so misunderstood
Now we're jumping at shadows with anxiety high
Not safe anymore, no matter how hard we try

We see the threats out there, imagined or not
Our faith in humanity has been totally shot
Minds full of anguish, of battles intense
Or of suicide bombers from which there is no defense

But we're not really crazy like everyone thinks
We just need some time to smooth out all those kinks
To adjust back to living in the land of the free
And somehow get a handle on our PTSD

So please don't consider us dangerous men
We just need some patience, we need a good friend

THOUGHTS AND REFLECTIONS

_____

_____

_____

_____

_____

_____

_____

_____

_____

_____

_____

_____

_____

_____

_____

_____

INVISIBLE WOUNDS

From waking in the dead of night,
with nightmares filled with endless fright
From sweating in a crowded room,
with morbid thoughts of pensive doom

From terrifying thoughts and dreams,
that fill our minds with silent screams
From pressure felt in chest and head,
with feelings of impending dread

From fears unjustified to those
whom never faced such deadly foes
From such dark places, our fear it flows
with anger matched, Heaven only knows

The hardship of living, day by day it grows
But from all of this we still strive to be,
what we were before crossing o'er the sea

Please understand it's not the life that we chose,
to have fear hang upon us like old, tattered clothes
To have shackled to us the pain and grief,
and yet forever hoping to find some relief

From our hearts to yours, may you please understand
this wasn't our dream, this life wasn't planned
though our visible scars may show the war we've been in
It's our invisible wounds that cuts deepest within.

THOUGHTS AND REFLECTIONS

QUESTIONS

Have you killed anyone?
Have you fired your gun?
Have you shot or been wounded?
Did you do it for fun?
Did you stab anyone with your
bayonet sharp?
Have you looked in one's eyes
as they faded to dark?

Have you suffered enough
from these questions they ask
Have you suffered them quietly
Or taken the asker to task?

Have you let them know
that it just isn't right?
Have you explained that their
questions
Bring you right back to the fight?

Have you stood there so silent
while the pain flows again?
And the questions keep firing
like the wind driven rain

To those who don't understand
it's so hard to explain
the wounds cutting deeper
and the grief and the pain

So the next time they ask
for what they think they should
know
Explain in short phrases
Take a breath, deep and slow

Tell them their knowledge
that they seek to gain
Is not worth the heartache
It's not worth the pain

For the memories you have
are not meant to be shared

and that they shouldn't ask
for answers they're not prepared

For though the burden is heavy
and their answers never known
You carry it for them
It's something you bear alone

THOUGHTS AND REFLECTIONS

_____

_____

_____

_____

_____

_____

_____

_____

_____

_____

_____

_____

_____

_____

_____

_____

_____

COMMON THREAT OF PTSD

It's not always bullets nor bombs bursting in air
It's not always shrapnel whizzing fast by your ear
It's not always the sound of the guns and grenades
It's not always the feeling of death coming in spades
It's not always the mortars, RPGs, IEDs
It's not always but it could be just some of these

It could also be events that were out of control
And you were the victim from which it has taken its toll
It could also be trauma that was too much to bear
And you suffered greatly from the worst kind of scare

Whatever the causes and whatever the reasons
I'm here for you always, a friend for all seasons
I've had my own kinds of trauma and my own little hell
and I suffer as you do, and others suffer as well

Our traumas have made us become what we are
As silent we fight what has no visible scar
Together we'll press on though, we'll stand the good fight
Our hands intertwined, they'll soon know our might

We'll work with each other with one common thread
Till the memories we're fighting are tamed in our head
We'll stand with each other and be there as friends
Till the nightmares inside us finally come to an end

THOUGHTS AND REFLECTIONS

MY DREAMS AND I

Alone at last, my dreams and I
till nightmares overtake us.
Strong we are, unafraid to die
till flashbacks try to break us.

I close my eyes and try to breathe
so pleasant dreams return here,
but memories, like eels they seethe
and creep in my mind with fear.

The shadows on the wall take form
like frightening ghosts and things
that swirl around as if a storm
with all the fear that brings

The whispers on the wind set sail
like demons sounds surrounding
in voices haunting, old and frail
with heartbeats loud and pounding

I tell myself it's in my mind
these torturous scenes and phrases
repeating mantras soft and kind
till peace, its head it raises

Then comes the nightmares once again
And my mind remains their evil playpen

THOUGHTS AND REFLECTIONS

THE SAND

The sandbox once my youthful friend
I played in daily to no end
My innocence could never dream
That sand, my nemesis, would seem
To rob me of my childhood faith
And bring the darkness like a wraith

It haunts me now like Satan's dust
Destroying all I'd come to trust
My hopes and dreams all scattered now
To defeated pride I humbly bow

Perhaps someday from that sand I'll build
A castle strong with faith fulfilled
But till that day I find that strength
I think I'd go to any length
To rid this curse of sand and wind
And bring the nightmares to an end

THOUGHTS AND REFLECTIONS

SHOPPING

His pulse is quickening
His nausea's sickening
His palms are sweating
His nerves upsetting

His eyes go hectic
With glances frantic
His stomach knots
With deep morbid thoughts

A deep, deep breath
And away goes Death
As the clerk says the price
"Do you want stamps or ice?"

His surroundings take form
Everything's back to the norm
There's no weapon in hand
No "take cover" command

He panicked again
when surrounded by men
But standing in line
At the old Five and Dime

No opponents were there...
But what was, was the FEAR
From a dark places it dwells
From deep terror it swells

And there's no other choice
But to give fear the voice
And try shopping again
When the crowd starts to thin

THOUGHTS AND REFLECTIONS

BRING IT

Restless demons full of fight
Torment me thru endless night
Spirits' screams are incoherent
Their purpose though is so apparent

Waking hours filled with fear
Distrust to all whom dared to near
Paranoia rears its' ugly head
Replacing hope with doubt and dread

I did not ask this for my life
To be wounded sharp by pain and strife
But I'd gladly bear the brunt of all
And proudly suffer standing tall

For my life was serving others first
So bring pain on and do your worst
You'll find though broken I will emerge
With nervous tension on the verge

I'll bear my scars as best I can
And with honor shining here I stand
Before you now I humbly try
To look you squarely in the eye

To tell you I, though tattered, torn
Will not mock you, will not scorn
I too feel pain, I feel the hurt
From playing in the "sand box" dirt

And gladly do it all again
With pain my partner, fear my friend
To rise each morning with pride and say
I'm here for you, and I'm here to stay

THOUGHTS AND REFLECTIONS

DREAMS

Tattered dreams, broken nights
Hours lost till morning lights
Sharp visions stab the inner eye
As nightmares clear, sun rises high

Memories full with brunt of strain
As sun dissolves in clouds of rain
Horror fills my thoughts for when
The time to sleep prepares again

THOUGHTS AND REFLECTIONS

_____

_____

_____

_____

_____

_____

_____

_____

_____

_____

_____

_____

_____

_____

_____

_____

_____

_____

PTSD

(written while in a mental ward)

We live medicated
"mental cases" we're called
For our wrath has hurt loved ones
And they, our actions appalled

To them, we're a stranger
Someone they never knew
For exposed once to danger,
O'er the cuckoo's nest we flew

We fly into rages
And sink into lows
And take ourselves places
That only heaven knows

But those that were wounded,
Lost an eye, leg or arm
Refuse to acknowledge us
Since there's no signs of harm

But I say to those wounded
Whom I hold honor and respect
They are the lucky ones
Their wounds found no neglect
They have something to show
For the sympathy vote
And look down on us
With a sneer and a gloat

I would rather have crutches
Or be wheelchair bound
Then live with this affliction
Only my mind carries 'round

THOUGHTS AND REFLECTIONS

SLEEP

Oh sleep, you have trumped me again
You have succeeded where I could not win
You have eluded my nights and altered my days
and I lay here defeated in so many ways

You've taken from me a night's long sleep
and the chance to ever fully slumber deep
You gave me nightmares when my eyelids were shut
and night sweats and terrors, it's a terrible rut

I tried to defeat you with various means
from numerous pills and CPAP machines
from warm milk, hot tea, or just water to drink
in hopes that in peaceful bliss, I would slink

Yet even now as I lay here at 2 in the morn
I curse at your name, your image I scorn
I take out my papers, I take out my pen
for traitorous sleep, you've beat me again.

THOUGHTS AND REFLECTIONS

_____

_____

_____

_____

_____

_____

_____

_____

_____

_____

_____

_____

_____

_____

_____

JUSTIFY ME
(Won Special Recognition Gold Medal In
The 2014 National Veterans Creative Arts Festival)

Give me a crutch
give me a cane
Just give me something
that shows for the pain
Give me a wound

Give me a scar
Just give me something
people can see from afar
To show that I'm wounded

To show I'm in pain
To show that I'm not
having it all in my brain
My wounds, they run deeply

But no-one can see
so please give me something
to justify me.
Please give me something ... to justify me.

THOUGHTS AND REFLECTIONS

TRIALS AND TRIED

From sweaty jungles and gritty sands
To stinking trenches in far off lands
From tunnels built for smallest man
To shrapnel skies in a flying can

Fighters, soldiers, sailors all
Have stood for us when heard the call
Some paid the price that war demands
Or made down payments with legs and hands

With determined chin they try to heal
But no one told them just how to feel
When coming home to peace and love
And to never fearing the skies above

To never need check behind each door
Or take a dive and hit the floor
When sounds so common to you and me
Fill that same vet with anxiety

The creaking floor, the coffeepot dripping
Could slowly start his facade to slipping
What once was calm and loving man
May have changed in him what he can't understand

And without more help, understanding and grace.....
That saddened troop may have to face
A jury of 12 that have no clue...
Of what PTSD and war can do to you

They'll convict without hearing all of the facts
And call him a Rambo because of his acts
The 12 would forget he would have laid down his life
For every one's mother, brother, sister and wife...

They'll sit on the court benches dictating his end
Till the gavel hammers in the final judgment to rend
And the life of a hero is cut short once again
But not from the actions in wars he's been in

You see War called the shots and it knew it would win
To a troop whose coming home was his only real sin.

THOUGHTS AND REFLECTIONS

WONDER

People often wonder
What it's like to be in pain
And people often wonder
Just what I have to gain

From pushing all those tiny pills
Down my throat each day
And seeing all the docs for ills
That never go away

In hearing thoughts from those like me
In discussion groups and therapy
I tell them this in honest prose
Don't wonder things only heaven knows

Don't wonder how I live or die
Or even wonder as to the why
But know this people, and know it well
Be glad I'm living in this hell

For you were spared this I live
From my giving all I had to give
For you in peaceful slumber sleep
While in my mind the nightmares creep

Your days are filled with joy and glee
While I suffer hardship stoically
And while though jealous I may be
Of living life so normally

So this I say to all that wonder
I'd once again put my life asunder
And fight in your place, let you stay home
To ponder my actions from within this poem

THOUGHTS AND REFLECTIONS

SCARS

Surgery scars, I have a few
Scars from youthful antics too
Scars that show my wilder side
Scars with shame I try and hide

But the deepest scars no one can see
Are the scars that dwell inside of me
The wounds though old, still hurt me so
As the painful feelings from them flow

As they reopen every night
They fill my mind through eyes shut tight
With Fear like blood seeping through the scabs
Though deep inside, their pain it stabs

It haunts me, taunts me, till my mind it screams
As these scars remember most traumatic scenes
Though through vivid dreams and waking scares
The scars aren't seen, so no one cares

But tho none can see these scars inside
They're a part of me that can't be denied
Their pain, their hurt, will never heal
Like oozing wounds that never seal
And though I pray I'll not succumb

These scars define who I've become
And though my life's not what I planned Scarred and
wounded, here I stand.

THOUGHTS AND REFLECTIONS

_____

_____

_____

_____

_____

_____

_____

_____

_____

_____

_____

_____

_____

_____

_____

STEVEN BATES

FLASHBACKS

Memories merging
Into
One

Nightmares purging
All the
Fun

Sacred prayers are said
In vain

As haunted eyes relive
The pain

As Sadness, Grief, and endless Horror
Flash silently in dreams abhorred
Then cries of anguish, doom, despair
Escape from lips into the air

As simple sounds disturb the night
Startling them with unknown fright
Dawn brings the sun, a fresh new day
Yet weary eyes can't look away

And ears can't deafen to the sounds
Of piercing tones from whistling rounds
Then smells return to fool the mind....
Of another place, another time

The burden's heavy and takes
its'
toll

To traumas burned
within
the soul

And as the pain refreshes, and hope
May fall

The scars may never show
At All.

62

THOUGHTS AND REFLECTIONS

PILLS

Pills for nightmares
Pills for bad scares
Pills to keep my mind in check
Pills to keep me from being a wreck

Pills that keep my body straight
Pills that keep me in a calming state
Pills to keep down pain and strife
Pills to keep up a happy life

Pills that help with all the twitching
Pills that help with all the itching
Pills that help my beating heart
Pills that help my breathing start

Pills for this, and pills for that
Pills for making me not so fat
Pills that do all but make me cry
Why all these pills, please tell me why

THOUGHTS AND REFLECTIONS

LIVING WITH PTSD

Therapy and psychotropic drugs
Inner peace and embracing hugs
Introspection, sharing pain
methods all to train the brain

Methods tried and methods failed
Methods yet to have success prevail
For helping us to find a way
to live like normal day to day

To make us fit in society
without our life as the enemy
Perhaps someday a method will work
and from our Life we will not shirk

But till that day of success we see
We'll struggle though living with PTSD

THOUGHTS AND REFLECTIONS

_____

_____

_____

_____

_____

_____

_____

_____

_____

_____

_____

_____

_____

_____

_____

8ᵀᴴ **FLOOR**

(Written while in the 8th floor Mental Ward in OKC)

The moans, the groans
The cries of pain
The fears of loss
And nothing to gain

The tears of sorrow
Anguish and grief
Pure anger and rage
Without any relief

Anxious and sweating
With nightmarish dreams
Guilt ridden and saddened
From their curses and screams

Shunning their family
Neighbor and friend
Knowing with others
Wounds they cause never mend

Alone and secluded
Is their preferred life to be
For crowds make them nervous
So to privacy they flee

Yes, these are our veterans
Some wounded in war
Who reside in the Psych ward
In the VA's 8ᵗʰ floor

THOUGHTS AND REFLECTIONS

_____

_____

_____

_____

_____

_____

_____

_____

_____

_____

_____

_____

_____

_____

PAIN

Pain and depression, they cut like a knife
And tears to the very heartbeat of life
They rip at the fabric of sanity and hope
And shreds peaceful living as it hangs by a rope

It carves out the joy that you once held so dear
And spits out the pieces both far and near
It grinds at the memories, erasing all dreams
Till the pain it brings forth explodes at the seams

It torments in nightmares, in the sounds all around
In the smells and the dust where it strives to be found
In reflections and flashes caught in the corner of eyes
The pain and depression fills our head full of lies

Paranoia then follows as swift as the wind
And our fears manifest till the night's bitter end
Then as we awaken with gasping for air
We struggle to realize the horrors aren't there

They're in the backs of our mind, they belong in the past
And we hope evermore that our symptoms won't last
We self-medicate with both liquor and drugs
Or ignore it completely sweeping it under the rug

We talk in our groups, or in therapy alone
Or when things turn real bad, then we pick up the phone
We call to the hotlines, to the psychics, or docs
Hoping each we reach out to finds the key that unlocks

To open the floodgates of gloom and despair
And release our burdens, set them free in the air
But alas the pain stays, though, forgotten at times
Till it ends up here as somebody's rhymes

So take all your pain, your depression and fears
And let me write of them, let me cry the tears
Let me be the voice of the pain that we share
Let me be the shoulder for the weight that you bear

Free up your burdens and smile once again
So Sayeth our Savior, in His name ...Amen

THOUGHTS AND REFLECTIONS

TO DREAM

To dream of peace instead of war,
or of nightmares frightening to the core
To dream of joy instead of hate,
or of heinous acts from evil innate

To dream of persons safe and sound
than those whom misery has tied and bound
To finally rest when eyes are closed
than see the horror our world exposed

To finally sleep with peaceful thoughts
instead of stomach wrenching knots
To finally wake with no regret
than lying in a pool of sweat

To finally sleep and get some rest
Is what I dream, it's what I quest
and till that day of final peace
I pray each day the nightmares cease

THOUGHTS AND REFLECTIONS

THE KNIGHT

My armor's on, my shield's in place
My demeanor is a stony face
My thoughts secure, my mask complete
My emotions hard as set concrete

My smile betraying the inner tears
Knowing no one now can see my fears
No one but me can see the pain
When persons ask without refrain

With questions wounding like arrows shot
About the past and battles fought
I would rather not talk or remember the past
I am crying inside while the memories last.

Yes, the "knight in shining armor" is here once again
just please don't ask what I've done, where I've been
It brings up old memories I'd rather have hid
and my armor's the only thing keeping a lid
on all the emotions, all of the pain.

My helmet is faceless, it conceals once again
the hideous beasts called guilt and despair.
Those dragons within me that none are aware,
torment and fight me in this metal skin.

Straining to burst free from this armor so thin
but they yield to me now as I learn how to cope
which is giving me courage, and giving me hope

THOUGHTS AND REFLECTIONS

_____

_____

_____

_____

_____

_____

_____

_____

_____

_____

_____

_____

_____

_____

SHADOWS

A shot rings out and I hit the floor
as shadows lurks behind each door
My eyes starts racing to find the foe
with furtive glances for where to go

As I crawl around I realize
I'm not where I have visualized
My mind sees things that are not there
still preying on my deepest fear

The shot I heard was just a car
but the shadows still as dark as tar

THOUGHTS AND REFLECTIONS

DARK THOUGHTS

SUICIDE AWARENESS

Cold metal blade against my wrist
Goodbyes said to all on my list
Slicing slowly, the pain not felt
Just another agony Life to me has dealt

I've lost all hope, my dreams are gone
While people said to "just move on"
They've no idea how low I am
Nor did they offer to give a damn

If only someone had seen the signs
If only someone had heard my whines
If only someone had said to me
"There are other ways to set you free.

There are places to go and people to call,
From people who know what it's like to fall"
Yes, the helpline call could have saved my life
I realize now, as I lay down my knife

Had someone else recognized my pain
For I was just too low and no hope remained
So look my brothers to those in need
And talk to them before they do the deed

For they only know the depth and despair
And need just one person to say "I care"

THOUGHTS AND REFLECTIONS

FINAL REGRET

Futile thoughts as suicide beckons
Sadness overwhelming, darkness deepens
Pointless living, depression sinking
Pity on me the primary thinking

No remorse, no guilty feeling
Morbid thoughts make Death appealing
No thoughts of loved ones, family, friend
One thought in mind, the goal, The End

My finger tightening, locked and loaded
A moment's flash, then all exploded
Now looking down, with regret I see
There were more important ones than me

THOUGHTS AND REFLECTIONS

HELPLINE HOPE

In desperate tones I silently screamed,
For nightmares and death were all I dreamed.
Behind my smiles my anguish reigned,
and I held in all in, as I'd been trained

It ate my soul, my every thought
My every hope, my dreams all shot
A reason to live was all I needed
Before the sparks of hope had all receded

So I called the number with one last sigh
A helpline desk that I gave a try
And though moments away was I from death
I told them all in one big breath

They listened to me with such devotion
That despair became a fleeting notion
I still feel down, don't get me wrong
and my pain is there, it's never gone

But now I know there is someone to hear
of the pain I have, of my despondent fear
There's always someone at the end of that line
To help find hope and peace of mind

So call them please when you spiral down
there's no better time, someone's <u>always</u> around

THOUGHTS AND REFLECTIONS

_____

_____

_____

_____

_____

_____

_____

_____

_____

_____

_____

_____

_____

_____

_____

_____

_____

_____

FINAL REMORSE

With one single action, I thought I'd be free
Now thinking back, it's with regret that I see
I was being selfish, so my thoughts would reflect
I didn't care whom my death would affect

I could not see my goal would only hurt others
And how my death would touch my sisters' and brothers'
If only I had talked or picked up a phone
And found there were more reasons than just me alone

More reasons to march on, more reasons to live
To boldly go on with my one life to give
My one life so it seems would affect so much more
Than just ending my suffering and closing that door

There are people who know me and people that care
And those to whom my passing would be totally unfair
My life's but a strand of a web so complex
That I never realized the number it affects

I now know the suffering that would have ended that day
Would cause so much more grief than any could say
My family and friends would all wonder why
And be torn all apart by my sudden goodbye

So with all due remorse to my most selfish of thought
I live proudly knowing that I caused no distraught
Yes my pain is intense and my suffering is real
But surviving is the first step to beginning to heal

So reach out to someone if you are considering
The Deed
And remember those loved ones…and to healing…
GODSPEED

THOUGHTS AND REFLECTIONS

SUICIDE HOTLINE POEM

In desperate times I've held the rope
In darkness black when I couldn't cope
In deep low places I've pulled the hammer
When despair and grief in silence clamor

When despondency brought me to the blade
And depression its final argument made
When all hope was lost and gave in I did
To the Final Deed which all forbid

Yet before the act a voice rang clear
Which reminded me about my fear
That it's not my life I would be taking
But the lives of loved ones I'd be forsaking

My pain would end but theirs would start
And I would leave them all with broken heart
No reason given, I'd just be gone
And do to them the greatest wrong

So yet in darkness there was still light
For which I struggled and fought the fight
I pulled myself up and found you can survive
By calling 1 800 273 8255

THOUGHTS AND REFLECTIONS

THE PATCH

A big man, with a voice cracking
Hugged me hard and tight
Spoke of courage he once was lacking
When he had given up the fight

His life it seemed was near the end
He was about to lose the battle
And deeply needed just a friend
Before he threw in the towel

He found inspiration in a poem I penned
An unexpected boost of courage
The will to press on and then contend
To his soul it gave advantage

And from his pocket he pulled a patch
And with trembling hand he held
This piece of cloth with Velcro latch
It was a treasure my eyes beheld

A half-moon face with a single teardrop
Facing three stars in sky blue backdrop
The Robin Williams Memorial Morale patch
...........And it means the world to me

THOUGHTS AND REFLECTIONS

LIFE

Alone in the dark,
Alone in the light
Just missing the mark,
Just missing outright

Failing at all things,
Failing affection
Heavy with yearnings,
Heavy depression

Trapped by confusion,
Trapped by delusion
Life's a contusion,
Life's an illusion

THOUGHTS AND REFLECTIONS

REMINDERS

A weekly test of a tornado alarm
Makes me duck and hide from harm
A simple car horn takes me back
To places where I fear attack

A slamming door and fireworks
Takes me where the danger lurks
Outside myself, no danger near
But in my mind I'm filled with fear

I look around and all I see
Are targets aiming back at me
I try to calm these aberrations
And that I'm not in those situations

I ground myself with three known facts
To remind me that I'm back, intact
And though this happens most every day
I still stand with pride and say

Though I've ventured places within my mind
A spark of sanity you'll find
That keeps me going and pressing on
Until the nightmares are said and gone

And though my fate's to relive the past
I'm still in control, the pain won't last

THOUGHTS AND REFLECTIONS

STOP ME

Wondering … Just thinking out loud if I can
Why is it my life that's sinking?
Is it some cosmic plan?

The depths that I'm dwelling
Seem to be to no end
And my protests and yelling
Bring no one to mend

I feel that there's no one
That understands my sorrow
And I doubt I'll see Sun
By this time tomorrow

All I need Is a person
A relative or friend
To rid this here toxin
And my depression upend

I know that can't cure me
Or stop my mind if it's set
But I know they'll assure me
Suicide's not my kismet

Just one little soul
One person I pray
Please stop my goal
Put my plan at bay

I don't care about who...
Please help change my mind
Maybe it's you
Just someone be kind

You just never know
Whose depression, they hide
And their darkness won't show
But they're right by your side

So smile today and make you a friend
For you never can say whose plans just might end
For if only you'd smile, perhaps just a wave
It might take a while, but a life you might save!

THOUGHTS AND REFLECTIONS

_____

_____

_____

_____

_____

_____

_____

_____

_____

_____

_____

_____

_____

_____

_____

_____

PATRIOTISM AND SECURITY POLICE PRIDE

BLUE BERET

Cold and lonely thru the night
sweating on guard thru day
always ready for the fight
whatever comes their way

Watching the distance for a threat,
alert to those nearby
Forever watching, without fret
with furtive glancing eye

Walking endless miles on post
their boots, the soles worn thin
Walking silent as a ghost
these trusted, stalwart men

They earned the right
to proudly say
I alone shall own the night
For I am a Blue Beret!

THOUGHTS AND REFLECTIONS

_____

_____

_____

_____

_____

_____

_____

_____

_____

_____

_____

_____

_____

_____

_____

_____

_____

_____

STEVEN BATES

MY OATH

Twelve years ago and I remember the day
My uniform came off and in mothballs did stay
My ribbons and rank, they no longer held sway
And my medals just dust gatherers in drawers as they lay

My badge and my shield stored along my beret
And the memories, like shadows, my mind holds at bay
But to the friendships I made, to my brethren, I say
My loyalty to you needs no reward and no pay

I swore to fight with you, beside you in the fray
To defend you and keep you from death's dark doorway
And I'll be there if needed, to my oath I'll obey
To you and my country, this U.S. of A

THOUGHTS AND REFLECTIONS

"SP" TO THE CORE

My body is shivering, while alone here I stand
With nothing for company, just my rifle in hand
Near my feet is my 'A' bag chock full of supplies
For any contingency, terrorist, or spies.

And I'll stand till relieved, or so that is the plan
But you can never quite count on the other flight's man
For I may stay till dawn, or till dusk falls once more
But I'll stand nonetheless, for I'm "SP" to the core!

THOUGHTS AND REFLECTIONS

MEMORIAL DAY

"Happy" is not something that I like to hear
with words like "Memorial Day", a sacred time of the year.
Why use the word "happy" on such a sad day
When we honor our veterans while in graveyards they lay.

We should use words like
"Honored', "Respectful", "Revered"
When we speak of all those that our nation interred.
We mourn on the day for those lives in war lost
and whose price for our freedom, the ultimate cost.

So I stand here, a veteran, while "Taps" plays and eyes cry
and I honor and revere those with whom angels now fly
Yes, "Happy" is not something I like to hear
but a "Respectful" Memorial Day to you,
and to those you hold dear.

THOUGHTS AND REFLECTIONS

STEVEN BATES

MOTTOS

Aim High ... Fly-Fight-Win's the cry
To Always Faithful, Semper Fi
And Anchors Aweigh, my friend
To the Army motto, "This we'll defend"

"Always Ready", The Coast Guard's pact
For these proud services, their honor's intact
With duty, courage, commitment too
They fight for freedom, they fight for you

They stand for freedom, they stand for peace
They stand forever, till wars they cease
Then they'll stand as deterrents to violent attacks
Whatever happens, America, they'll have our backs

So if you should meet one of our nations' pride
Remember their mottos with which they abide
And think long and hard on the sacrifice made
Their blood spilt in war, the cost that they paid
For a motto's an oath and an oath they obeyed

THOUGHTS AND REFLECTIONS

DEBT

On Veteran's Day we honor those
With whom evil countries we did oppose
With whom we sent in danger's way
Who fought for freedom, never swayed

Who fought and bled and died for peace
So good may live and evil cease
We honor those for whom we owe
Our very lives that made them go

And fight for freedom, yours and mine
And Liberty, a gift Divine
No greater love, no greater gift
Gave those who died, to those that lived

So thank them softly with whispered prayer
And hope your children also hear
That to those brave souls we owe a Debt
We honor those we call …a Vet

THOUGHTS AND REFLECTIONS

_____

_____

_____

_____

_____

_____

_____

_____

_____

_____

_____

_____

_____

_____

_____

_____

_____

ODE TO OLD GLORY
*(Written For A Boy Scout Troop On 4th Of July 2014
For A Flag Retirement Ceremony)*

She's flown over battles
Over conflicts and wars
She's flown over deserts
And the deadliest shores

She's flown high for freedom
This red, white and blue
But for this certain flag
Her time now is through

She'll no longer fly
Over this land that we love
She'll no longer soar
On a mast high above

She'll no longer wave
Over this land of the free
But she'll fly in our hearts
As a fond memory

THOUGHTS AND REFLECTIONS

STANDING WATCH

Trudging forward day and night
like slaughter driven cattle.
Loaded down with all the gear
perchance there is a battle.

Standing tall and guarding all
and holding ever fast.
Never knowing day by day
if this will be our last.

Yet our honor will not falter
and our duties we will keep.
Firmly standing watch o'er others,
while they restless sleep.

THOUGHTS AND REFLECTIONS

_____

_____

_____

_____

_____

_____

_____

_____

_____

_____

_____

_____

_____

_____

_____

_____

_____

_____

_____

THOUGHTS FROM THE HEART

OFFICER DOWN

"Officer Down", those chilling words
That strike a spouse to the core.
And a family waits, and prays upwards
For the news to tell them more.

Was it their Beloved Father, Son,
Mother, Daughter, Husband, Wife
That leaves the job this day undone
And gave it all, up to their life

For a shooter may have fired that gun
Or a car spun out of control
Or any reason under the sun
Whose actions took their toll

"Officer Down" repeated again
On the news, the web, in print
While frantic calls to next of kin
To find which home was sent

A patrol car with a team in blues
And black stripe upon their shield
To knock upon the door with news
That the loved one had been killed

"Officer Down", those words strike fear
For another's life was taken,
A life whose job they held so dear
To make our country safe in

A life that trained to keep the peace
And keep the bad at bay
But an "officer down" to all police
Means family died today

REFLECTIONS OF A BERET

THOUGHTS AND REFLECTIONS

STONE CYCLONE

Pelting stones with dust and dirt
Flying rocks bring pain and hurt
Circling round and crashing hard
As wounds bleed free from every shard

Gusting winds spin round and round
As marble chunks to flesh do pound
But the winds are thoughts, each stone a word
That flail with hate and pain when heard

The cyclone vicious attacks in deed
As scars from past assaults do bleed
The suffering intense as curses fly
While hope prevails that anger die

The cyclone's raging, but faith flows strong
For the storm to break like morning dawn
Perhaps peace may still a calm abet
And pray the stones go silent yet

THOUGHTS AND REFLECTIONS

YOUR VOICE

Of all the songs that have been sung,
Of the bells and chimes that I've heard rung
Of the gentle winds from North and South
That blows so soft from Heaven's Mouth

From the gentle coo of the turtledove
As he flits with mates in skies above
Of all these sounds I may have heard
Be they made by man, by wind or bird

There is none so sweet as that which slips
From the prison walls of your ruby lips
For angels, perched on clouds aloft
In shame keep harps strings silent, soft

In hopes with luck someday they'd hear
Your sweet soft voice they hold so dear.

THOUGHTS AND REFLECTIONS

_____

_____

_____

_____

_____

_____

_____

_____

_____

_____

_____

_____

_____

_____

_____

_____

_____

_____

LET ME

Let me look into your eyes
As sparkling seas they seem
To take me to a far off place
That fills my highest dream.

Let me press against your mouth
These lonely lips of mine
Which thru the evening cry out loud
And thru the sunlight whine

Let me once, and only once
Touch your fine physique,
Which sends my head a'spinning round
And makes my body weak.

For it is these things I'd love to do
And girl, you know with who.
For there's nothing more I'd rather say,
Than, "Sweetheart, I Love You!"

THOUGHTS AND REFLECTIONS

ALWAYS AND FOREVER

Always and Forever,
that is my love for you
"No matter what" is added
To prove my love is true

"With all my heart and soul" I say
to prove my love runs deep
and Love won't wander, fade away
or vanish in my sleep.

I wake each morning more in love
That's how my days begin
And love grows stronger every day
till sunset brings day's end

And as I sleep once more love grows
for you ..my love... my friend.

THOUGHTS AND REFLECTIONS

SONNET OF A FATHER

To be a father of a little girl
to be her mentor guiding her thru life
her protector in this wild crazy world
and giving her away to be a wife

Though never letting go, the bond still tied forever
watching , waiting for her call
to be the one comes running to her side
to pick her up perchance that she should fall

To brush her off and stand her on her own loving
her regardless is your duty
supporting her though now she's old and grown
forever being there despite the fee

A father always, mentor, and her friend
To be there for her to the very end

THOUGHTS AND REFLECTIONS

_____

_____

_____

_____

_____

_____

_____

_____

_____

_____

_____

_____

_____

_____

_____

_____

_____

_____

WEDDING BLESSING

Hearts entwined like shadows merged at sundown,
with hopes and dreams combined for love to share.
Soul mate searches ended with no letdown,
for love has merged the two from once a pair

Unified as one they both endeavor
to live as one in harmony and peace
knowing that their love will last forever
and love will always blossom , never cease.

Companions till end of time they promise
to hold each other, sickness and in health
In diversity , turmoil and calmness
for better, worse, poorer or in wealth

So may love and joy guide them thru all tests
and be a couple now forever blessed

THOUGHTS AND REFLECTIONS

_____

_____

_____

_____

_____

_____

_____

_____

_____

_____

_____

_____

_____

_____

_____

_____

_____

_____

_____

FIRST YEAR

Though the year has been rough
And hard to endure
And the budget's been tough
With no easy cure

Though our stress level's risen
To heights unsurpassed
And the spark has been fizzin'
From being lied to, harassed

Though our lives became cluttered
With worries and care
And sarcasm's oft muttered
When our tempers, they flare

Though it seems that the hardship
Overfloweth our cup
It's only strengthened our friendship
So that I'll never give up

For you see, you're the bond
Holding the cracks in my life
And I couldn't go on without you as my wife
For your beauty and love

Are still treasures I crave
For you were sent from above
An angel...for a knave

I love you more this day
Than any day in my past
And I hope and I pray
That our marriage will last

THOUGHTS AND REFLECTIONS

NOTHING BETWEEN US

Nothing between us but love and desire
Nothing between us but fuel for the fire
Nothing between us, no secrets, no lies
Nothing between us, no deception or guise

Nothing between us, no harbored ill will
Nothing between us, no shoulder of chill
Nothing between us, no words left un-spoke
Nothing between us, no curse to invoke

Nothing between us, no burdens to hide
Nothing between us, just arms open wide
Nothing between us, just this one thing is true
Nothing between us, just my love for you.

THOUGHTS AND REFLECTIONS

LOVE

No speech can convey
Nor artist can paint
No words can relay
Nor memories taint

No songs can compare
Nor poems relate
No thoughts of despair
Nor harshness abate

For my love is so pure
Indescribably so
And nothing's so sure
Except letting you know

For my heart is so heavy
With hoping you'd see
That just once I can tell thee
How great love can be

THOUGHTS AND REFLECTIONS

_____

_____

_____

_____

_____

_____

_____

_____

_____

_____

_____

_____

_____

_____

_____

_____

_____

_____

FOREVER

Another day and next to her I wake
My love so deepened even as I slept
Her heart and soul she gladly had me take
For in her breasts my love she kept

Our love a truly wondrous bit of fate
That sealed a destiny of hearts to share
And though our lives on Earth will soon abate
In Heaven we shall last forever there

Forever caring, forever loving
Forever holding and forever whole
Forever part of each other's being
Forever a part of each other's soul
Forever a love our hearts will entwine
Forever I am hers….and she is mine

THOUGHTS AND REFLECTIONS

HER LOVE

For once in my life there's someone for me,
Who cares for my feelings, my thoughts, my dreams
With a love that's so honest, with love so free
Without any traps, without any schemes

A love that's so precious, a love so rare
A love unpretentious, true love divine
A love full of joy, of hope and of care
That flows ever sweet to this heart of mine

Her love is pure music, a sweet symphony
A chorus from Heaven, angles dare sing
While plucking harp strings in soft harmony
Echoing gently as church bells doth ring

For long in my life there was something amiss
Till now in my life, and I found True Love's kiss

THOUGHTS AND REFLECTIONS

MY ANGEL

Lying beside her as softly she dreams
I thank the Heavens that sent her to me
For as she sleeps I know that it seems
The stars shone brighter when she came to be

As gently does her breathing rise and fall
The angels quiet harp strings for her sighs
And when she wakes and gives the day her all
It seems the very world begins to rise

For nature bows her head when my angel awakes
And beckons birds to sing in glorious praise
The sun caresses her softly as daylight breaks
And looks upon her face with loving grace

This angel I know was truly meant
To be the blessing that Heaven to me sent

THOUGHTS AND REFLECTIONS

MY GREED

Treasures, desires, wants and needs
It's not for any that my heart bleeds
It's not for riches, nor for wealth
It's not for fitness, or good health

It's not for memories, good or bad
It's not for happy times or sad
My only dream is to see your smiles
And for that I'd gladly walk the miles

From one far end of the Earth across
I'd crawl bare kneed as my albatross
If only to have your eyes look down
And upturn a smile from your saddened frown

If only to hear a small sigh of relief
Easing your burdens like the wind takes a leaf
It's for this small treasure, a mere smile from you
That fills me with gladness, with joy I renew

My quest now is over but if, my love, you'd allow I'll
start it all over beginning with now

THOUGHTS AND REFLECTIONS

THE END

No greater heartache ever have I
Than watching our country just wither and die
Quickly decaying and rotting within
It pains me to say that this is the End

The end of the freedoms we loved as young children
The end of the passions grown wild with abandon
The end of our faith in our leaders to lead
The end of our pride in Democracy's creed

The Bill of Rights ended by courts and their flaws
The Constitution ended by Executive laws
Christian faith ended by forced conformation
No matter this country had Christian foundation

Feelings of tension sparked in racial relations
Instead of the melting pot that formed our great nation
The fear of "offending" silences open complaints
And fear of racism, our free speech it taints

We fear being shot, stabbed, or otherwise injured
As killers walk free and illegals are pampered
Whatever happened to this Nation so great,
That feeds on itself now with venom and hate?

So stand and support those whom oppose where we're going
Be counted as warriors to fight this evil that's growing
For if no one stops this course soon, my friend
Then sadly I say that this is...... the End

THOUGHTS AND REFLECTIONS

STEVEN BATES

FINAL THOUGHTS

THE COST OF LOYALTY
(Written While Guarding Two F-16s That Crashed in Spain)

Before me lies wreckage
Of two planes that once flew
But the bodies are missing,
Of those brave men in blue

One will stay buried
For he was found dead
The other was lucky
For he came out ahead

But what was the price
that they both had to pay?
They were willing to give life,
for their country, away.

And not just their life,
but their family and friends
Which proves that with loyalty,
The cost never ends.

THOUGHTS AND REFLECTIONS

WHAT WILL BE MOURNED?
(Written While Guarding Two F-16s That Crashed In Spain)

One pilot lies aching
From sunup till dawn
The other was lucky,
For his misery is gone

Yet both flew with courage
And both paid a cost
And their country will mourn
For the loved ones they lost

Yes, family will mourn for the man, not machine,
But Congress, Lord help them, grieve a lost F-16.

THOUGHTS AND REFLECTIONS

BLACK METAL AND ASHES

(Written While Guarding Two F-16s That Crashed In Spain)

Black metal and ashes
Were all that were found
As I looked at the carnage
Of a mighty bird downed

And I thought of the cost
That the taxpayers bore
And the men that were lost
Who no longer will soar

Yes, the blue sky was darkened
And the Earth painted black
By a plane daring the heavens
To claim a life back.

THOUGHTS AND REFLECTIONS

BACKSTAB

From where is the knife being plunged?
A bladed opponent that lunged?
Or was it a friend that attacks?
And twists ever slow in our backs?

Was the cut made by one we fight,
With bayonet flashing in the night?
Or was it from one that we trust?
That pierced ever fierce with bloodlust?

Which one has stabbed to the core,
and ended our life ever more?
Was it one with the scowl that we spied?
Or the menacing grin by our side?

Was it foe that had cut so precise
as to cut to the bone with each slice?
Was it part of the ones we call foes
whose evil and hate we oppose?

Or was it someone we trust in the end
who went with the guise of a friend?
In the end does it matter at all
as stiffly in death do we fall,
from whom the final wound made?
as the gravedigger turns over his spade

THOUGHTS AND REFLECTIONS

MEASURE OF A MAN

We use rulers and tape measures
To find a man's height and width
Of our airman and soldiers
To see if they're fit
But how do we find

If they truly add up?
Do we measure their mind?
Or how their chin's tilted up?
Do we count each and every
Single hair on their chest?

Or how do we abjectly
Know that they'll pass the test?
When thrown in the midst
Of a terrible battle

Will their courage be blitzed?
Or will they show their true mettle?
So how do we measure the true worth of a man?
How can it be known of his heart and his mind?

How can his actions in combat be certain?
How in the Earth do these answers we find?
How is the question, for so many years we have quested
But fact is, there's no answer till that man has been tested.

THOUGHTS AND REFLECTIONS

THE Z MONSTER
(Written While Performing Duties at Torrejon AB, Spain)

You stand alone at your post,
with your boots highly shined
but soft as a ghost
sleep creeps through your mind

It taunts you with scenery
of beds with cool sheets,
of fields and their greenery
where the sun warmly beats

You nod off for a second,
which soon becomes two
For the sleep, it has beckoned,
And the Z-Monster's got you!

THOUGHTS AND REFLECTIONS

A FAN'S EYES

With dry eyes misting
and smiles turned from frowns,
Our hearts were lifted and our spirits soared
And filled with such joy that sorrow it drowns
Our hearts growing happy as blessings poured

Softly muttering words of grateful praise
Thankful to be living in times like these
Thankful to witness such glorious days
Falling in adulation down to our knees

Laughter echoing till tears they did fall
Elation flowing like waves on the sea
Cheers from our lips and relatives we call
Pride washing over our near endless glee.

So what brought such joy to the depths of our soul?
The fact the Broncos won the Super Bowl!!

THOUGHTS AND REFLECTIONS

FALL

Crispy leaves on hardened ground
Lightly frosted with evening's snow
Crunching slightly with crackling sound
As gentle fall winds blow

Trees now naked bare their souls
And bow to Nature's bellows
As there lies beneath their boughs
Colors muted, reds and yellows

The air frosty, briskly nipping
As cheeks turn rosy red
The hell with this, my curses slipping...
I'm heading back to bed!

THOUGHTS AND REFLECTIONS

JOY

Torment and rage
Unbridled Fury
My mind cannot gauge.
My heart filled with worry.

No symptoms that show,
This horrendous feeling.
And no one could know.
How Senses are reeling.

Thoughts racing swiftly,
With no anchored tie.
Please someone tell me
I'm not supposed to die.

Then a calm still old voice
And a thought rushes in.
Saying I do have a choice
For He died for my sin.

My heart slowing down now
My mind under control
Peace found me somehow
For He's in my soul!

THOUGHTS AND REFLECTIONS

_____

_____

_____

_____

_____

_____

_____

_____

_____

_____

_____

_____

_____

_____

_____

_____

_____

_____

_____

STEVEN BATES

PHYSICAL THERAPY

Crippling pain it seizes me
My knee in hobbling agony
Bursitis, arthritis, meniscus tear
I swear my body is beyond repair

But physical therapy is the cure they say
Just do it at home only three times a day
"Come in for a visit we'll wrap it in heat"
"We'll poke you and prod you,
now wont' that be neat?"

Then stretching and walking
is what they have planned
Had I wanted torture I'd have stayed in the sand

THOUGHTS AND REFLECTIONS

PURPOSE

Tattered and torn, shred to pieces I am
An emptied husk, just a shell of a man
A vessel that's poured all its' contents away
A withered tree limb too dried up to sway

A hollowed out acorn from worms and decay
A rusted old pickup with no bed to lay
A decrepit old house with no floors or walls
A crumbling suit from forgotten mothballs

But yet in the darkness, the mold and fungi
I realize my purpose, my reason to cry
It's not to bemoan my poor, perilous plight
But to show other peers that there still is a light

At the end of the tunnel, around that last bend
Is the glow from the One, the One we call a friend
His patience unending, He knows when we'll come
As he reminds us our value is more than the sum

Of all of those pieces, the remnants of us
Of the parts left behind in the billowing dust
For we still left a trail through this thing we call life
And impacted others, whether husband or wife

Our lives did have purpose,
our lives did mean much
For our lifetime was filled giving others a touch
A touch of our spirit, a touch of our soul
That was our mission, that was our role.

We changed the entirety of the world that we knew
By a smile, or a grin, and a helping hand to a few
Our lives weren't so wasted is what I finally realize
I just wasn't aware of the scope and the size

So even now, reader, as I am nearing the end
I am filled once again, and you can call me a friend.

THOUGHTS AND REFLECTIONS

THE EAGLES PATH

A young cub he was when first he started
then from the Webelos he departed
His arrow of light shining on display,
he went on to live the Boy Scout way

He tread the trail to 1st Class rank
and from his Oath he dared not shrank
Earning badges thru hard work
and from the Law he didn't shirk

Till one day finally he met the goal
and stood proudly with the Eagle role
My eyes teared up and I swelled with pride
as I thought to myself of the long hard ride

And as I watched him standing tall
my son, the Eagle, no longer small
from the Cub he was till now all grown
He's made it all, all on his own

THOUGHTS AND REFLECTIONS

ARROWMEN

Elected by peers
Earned through Ordeal
Overcoming their fears
Now pride they should feel

An "Arrowman" by name
From leading by example
Seeking not status or fame
Just the honor is ample

To wear the sash of white
with an arrow of red
Is a privilege by right
To show others they've led

Then Brotherhood bound
Our Arrowmen strive
Till Vigil they've found
And completed their drive

Yes, the Arrowman's not lightly given
It's earned by sweat and work
And once your name is bidden
From your honor dare not shirk

THOUGHTS AND REFLECTIONS

CHRISTMAS

Tis a time for joy and time for cheer
This magical, wonderful time of the year
But there are those to whom
this time of year brings such pain
There are those for whom this time has
nothing to gain

There are those for whom this holiday season
Brings them down so low for no obvious reason
But the pain felt is real, it's not fake or imagined
The depression's is there, so deep and impassioned

The emptiness felt is so dark, so intense
For these poor souls there's no simple defense
It's not their choice that they feel so low
It's not their will to the depths they do go

It's not their fault and not just their choice
That the pain they have can't come to a voice
It nestles inside and silently simmers
Without any hope, no sparks, no glimmers

No way to say what's on their mind
No peace they know, no joy to find
So look to these others this joyous time
Help them find laughter and peace so sublime

The season is not about "getting" you see
It's all about giving to those so lonely
You'll find that your happiness
can come from within
If you just be there for them, a listener, a friend

And that is my only Christmas wish to you all
Is to help other people to stand and be tall
To rise from the bottom, to reach a new height
And Merry Christmas to ALL...
and to ALL a good night.

THOUGHTS AND REFLECTIONS

MEMORY

A thought quick approaches
Then nay, but it's gone
Another encroaches
But not for too long

My thoughts, they are scattered
My mind just half there
My memory's tattered
Tis my cross to bear

For the pain in my body
I've meds, pills galore
But the wound they can't see
Is the mind works no more

My ideas quickly fade
And my history is spent
And the memories I've made
I've no idea where they went

But the words that I cling to
Are on the tip of my tongue
Is a phrase I once knew
But alas, now it's gone

So listen my brothers
And my sisters heed too
Hear me all mothers
I'm talking to you

My point to this poem
Is clearly intended
And the rhyme, so ad nauseum
Be glad now has....ummm what was I saying?

THOUGHTS AND REFLECTIONS

HOPE

"Tomorrow is a brighter day"
(or so all the happy people say)
But what of those that are not so cheery
for them the day seems dark and bleary

Another day to feel the gloom
of heavy thoughts, impending doom
Of dreary nights so all alone
with joy so rare, nay, even unknown

Without a smile, without a dream
without a goal or self-esteem
without a cause or plan for life
without the love of a caring wife

To those that feel so sad and blue
I have this phrase to say to you
Remember no matter how lost, no matter how strange
At least you didn't vote for CHANGE!!!

THOUGHTS AND REFLECTIONS

PRAY FOR PARIS, PRAY FOR THE WORLD

A tragedy befell the world
With epitaphs of Allah hurled
The ISIS terror struck as cowards
Innocent lives by scores were tattered

Borders closed and traffic ceased
In search of those whom terror pleased
Soft targets killed, for they sought them out
While a President claimed he had his doubts

Of whom to blame this unholy act
But All were Muslims, that part is fact
And so begins the reign of terror
By those we welcomed home in error

Refugees, they called them that
Who upon our freedoms they did spat
And destroyed our nation from within
As horror spread with evil men

First the Christians died in vain
As swords fell swiftly with deep disdain
While others ignored the impassioned pleas
More non-Muslims fell on their knees

So now the question is where to strike
When friends and foes all look alike
So Pray for Paris, pray for the world
And keep Freedom's flag on high, unfurled

THOUGHTS AND REFLECTIONS

_____

_____

_____

_____

_____

_____

_____

_____

_____

_____

_____

_____

_____

_____

_____

_____

_____

SINNERS AND SAINTS

I'm paraphrasing just so you know
That my halo has long since lost its' glow
But how sad it is to hear and see
That those with different ideology

Can quote you scripture and expound
To try and turn your beliefs around
Forgetting that in the final days
It's foretold that this would be their ways

They know the Bible inside out
and recite it thinking they hold clout
But they themselves are doomed to be
Stuck on Earth for World War Three

So while they chant for religious "equality"
With the exception, though, of Christianity
For there's no place for God inside their hearts
A tragedy when the shooting starts

For Heaven would take them if only they'd see
The power of Christ in you and me
For though we aren't all committed as some
There is an End and it soon will come

So keep the Faith my fellow man
This time on Earth is nigh at hand
So forgive the sinners and their mistakes
This game is played at the highest stakes

But to God above it's not a game
So I'll leave you with that, in Jesus' name

THOUGHTS AND REFLECTIONS

FIBRO

Today I hope
To be pain free
Today I hope
For tranquility

Today I hope
To move with ease
Today I hope
God hears my pleas

Today I hope
But to no avail
For today's another
Hopeless day in Hell

THOUGHTS AND REFLECTIONS

―――――――――――――――

―――――――――――――――

―――――――――――――――

―――――――――――――――

―――――――――――――――

―――――――――――――――

―――――――――――――――

―――――――――――――――

―――――――――――――――

―――――――――――――――

―――――――――――――――

―――――――――――――――

―――――――――――――――

―――――――――――――――

―――――――――――――――

―――――――――――――――

―――――――――――――――

FOUR WORDS

As we sat there hearing the doctor's spiel About
options explored, decisions to fix
With methods to cure, solutions to heal
Chemotherapy chosen from all of the mix

With outlook cheerful and prognosis good
PET scans next to show the cancerous growth
In walked a vet worn as weathered wood
Nine times had he conquered this thing we loath

And he looked into our Father's eyes
And said four words that sent chills down spines
Yet giving hope his four words caught surprise
For in them courage came and dry eyes shines

His words, but four, now a challenge seated
His words, but four, said he ...."You CAN beat it"

THOUGHTS AND REFLECTIONS

LARRY - (ODE TO MY FATHER IN LAW)

I met him first a few years back
With my long hair flowing down
And I could tell he cut no slack
From the expression in his frown

But he honored me by shaking hands
And treating me with fairness
And I knew at once I liked the man
And he had a certain rareness

And I learned that he had lived his life
On the right side of the law
And I learned he'd seen his share of strife
And earned respect and awe

For he was not just my spouse's dad
And a father to his children
But a man whose very life had had
A reason for his living

And I learned from him a great many deal
Of kindness, strength and honor
And as I saw him lying still
I was proud he was our father

For though his life was snatched from us
and he was taken way too early
I found in him a man I could trust
And it was an honor knowing Larry

THOUGHTS AND REFLECTIONS

REFLECTIONS OF A BERET

About the Author

Born in Aurora, Colorado into an Air Force military family, Steven Bates began a traveling life very early. Shortly after his birth, his father was assigned to the Philippine Islands and a variety of locations after that, including a stint in Vietnam. In 1978 Steven's family was moved to Wiesbaden, West Germany, where they remained for 6 years. In 1984, Steven graduated from Gen. H.H. Arnold High School.

Steven began writing poetry in high school but rarely showed anyone his work, thinking it too unimpressive. Upon return to the United States, Steven began work as a night porter (janitor) at a Burger King in Panama City, Florida. He then took a turn working construction and siding with his brother-in-law in Oklahoma but realized the military or police work was what he really wanted to do, with the hopes of someday outranking his father.

Outranking his father in itself would be a challenge since his father was a Chief Master Sgt and the highest rank one could achieve as an enlisted man (E-9). Steven knew he needed college first and entered the Air Force Reserves in Dec 1985 as a Security Police Security Specialist. Enlisting in the Air Force Reserves would allow a way he could serve and have a way to pay for the college he needed.

His unit, the 919th Special Operations Squadron, not only gave him the means for starting college but gave him an opportunity to visit many unique locations to include Torrejon Air Base in Spain. Steven's participation in this unit introduced him to quite a variety of special weapons and tactics which served him well in later adventures. In his civilian life, Steven started work as a security officer for many different locations around Bay County, Florida.

The following year, in 1986, Steven attended the Law Enforcement Basic Standards course, earning Top Gun of his graduating class. After graduation, Steven applied to and accepted a Police Officer position in the Panama City Police Department. Steven served the community as a Police Officer for almost a year. Steven realized the difficulty of being a full time college student and working 12 hour shifts almost immediately and resigned from the department to finish his college. After leaving the Panama City Police Department, Steven entered the Correctional Officer Basic Standards course. Steven then took a position as a Correctional Officer for Corrections Corp of America at the Bay County Jail, which put his college on hold again.

Married by now, Steven knew he wasn't living up to his full potential and sought to enter the Air Force on active duty. Leaving the Air Force Reserves and going to the active duty Air Force meant a reduction in rank from the Staff Sergeant Fire Team Leader position he held in the Reserves. Taking the reduction in rank to an Airman First Class, E-3, rank did not deter him.

Steven entered the active duty Air Force in December 1989. His first assignment was the 2nd Bomb Wing at Barksdale AFB in Shreveport, Louisiana. From there, he deployed to Desert Shield in August 1990 as one of the first units to deploy to the "sandbox".

During that mission, Steven realized how the poems he wrote were becoming a catharsis not only to help him deal with the issues of deployment but were helping his fellow airmen as well. Steven began writing poems for his fellow airmen to send to their wives. Steven would often post inspirational poems on the bulletin boards to help others, and himself, in dealing with the difficulties of pending war.

When he returned to the United States, Steven immersed himself in being the best Airman he could be, but unfortunately by 1995 was starting to show signs of PTSD. Steven deployed to the 8th Security Police Squadron in South Korea that year as a Stinger Missile Operator. For such a specialized positon, Steven went through intense training at Fort Bliss, Texas. The unity and team camaraderie that Steven experienced in the Stinger unit was something Steven had not experienced since Desert Shield and with his old unit, the 919th.

That solidarity made quite the impact in bringing repressed and deep seated issues to the forefront. Steven began having sleepless nights and nightmares. When Steven went to the base doctor, a diagnosis of PTSD was not even entertained, so the doctor merely prescribed sleeping pills. Not recognizing this was the onset of PTSD, Steven returned to duty assuming the doctor was correct.

Steven's next assignment was with several units at F.E. Warren AFB in Cheyenne, Wyoming. It was during that time Steven went through another incident which further triggered his post-traumatic stress.

While visiting his two sons from a previous marriage in Phoenix, Arizona, Steven, along with his wife and daughter, was mistakenly identified by local law enforcement as driving a stolen vehicle. Steven, his wife and daughter, were surrounded by over a dozen law enforcement officers with guns aimed at him and at one point, at his 7-year daughter.

This incident amplified the sense of despair and helplessness and magnified the trauma of things he had already experienced. Steven was medically discharged from the Air Force in 2003, just short of one more hitch to achieve his 20 years in service.

Steven is a Disabled Veteran and lives with his wife, Sandy, in Cheyenne, Wyoming along with five assorted mutts and one cat.

Made in the USA
Columbia, SC
08 March 2021